WINTER IS HERE!

by Kimberly Weinberger
Illustrated by Jill Dubin

SCHOLASTIC INC.

New York   Toronto   London   Auckland   Sydney

For Karen, who likes big words
—K.W.

To Clark with love
—J.D.

Text copyright © 1997 by Scholastic Inc.
Illustrations copyright © 1997 by Jill Dubin.
All rights reserved. Published by Scholastic Inc.
CARTWHEEL BOOKS and the CARTWHEEL BOOKS logo
are trademarks and/or registered trademarks of Scholastic Inc.

ISBN 0-590-11507-3

10 9 8 7 6 5 4 3 2 1   7 8 9/9 0/0 01 02

Printed in the U.S.A.   24

First printing, December 1997

Winter is here!
Animals hide.

We dress in warm clothes.

We run outside.

Winter is here!

Snowflakes fall.

Touch them. Taste them.

Make a big ball.

Winter is here!

We skate. We sled.

We put a hat

on our snowman's head.

Winter is here!

We slip. We slide.

We can't wait
to go back outside!

Trains

Byron Barton

SCHOLASTIC INC.

New York   Toronto   London   Auckland   Sydney
Mexico City   New Delhi   Hong Kong   Buenos Aires

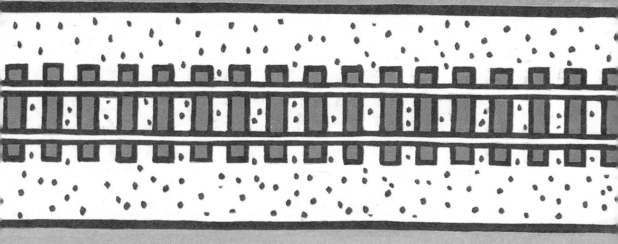

ISBN 0-439-47143-5

12 11 10 9 8 7 6 5 4 3 2   3 4 5 6 7 8/0

Printed in the U.S.A.   08

First Scholastic printing, April 2003

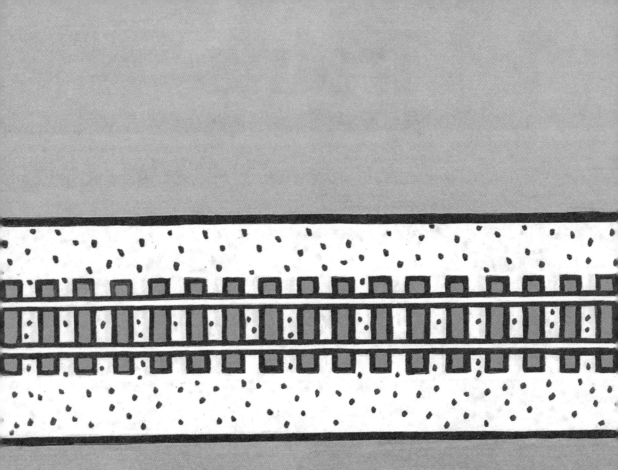

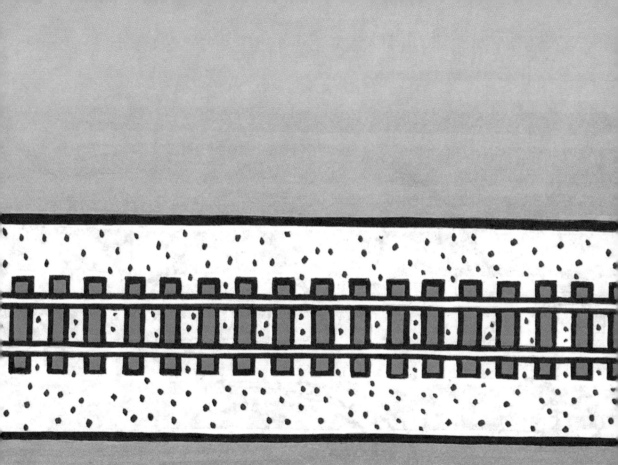

On the track

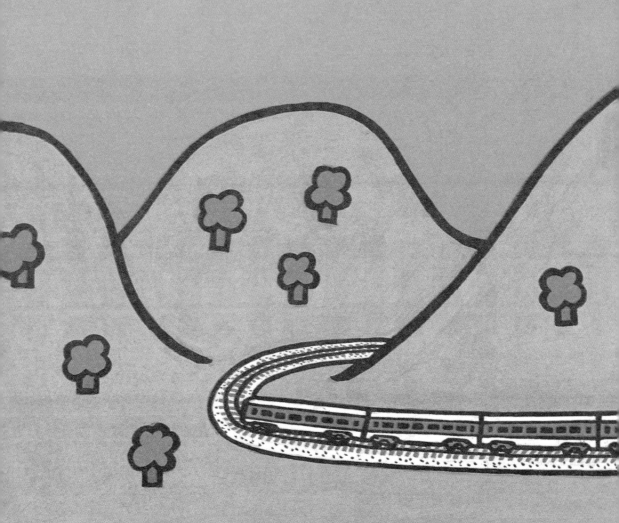

the trains are running.

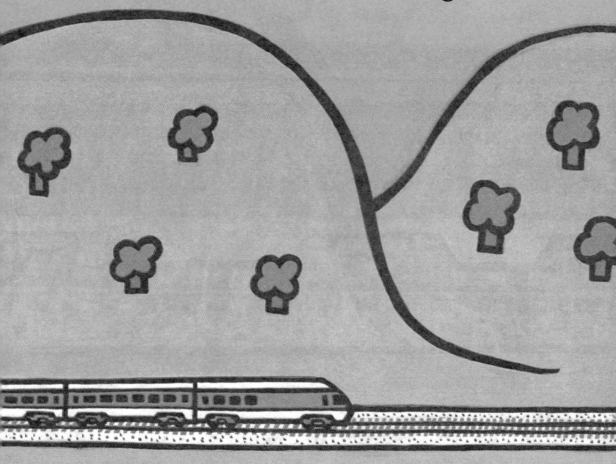

Here is a train

with people inside.

There goes a freight train

loaded with freight.

Here are the freight cars.

The caboose is last.

Here is a steam engine

puffing smoke.

There is an electric train.

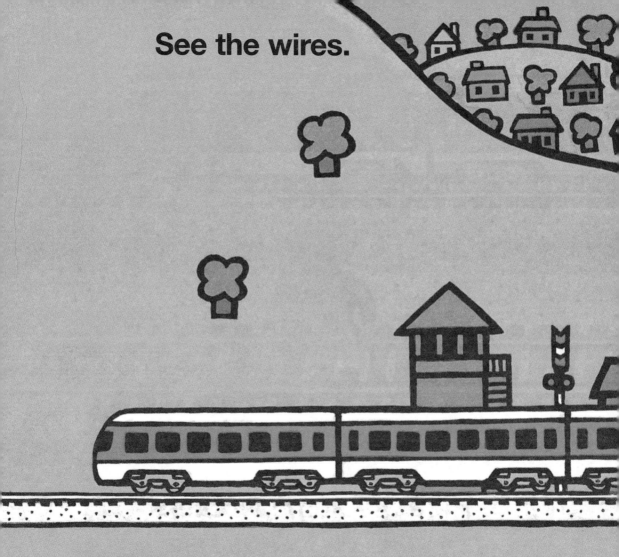

See the wires.

Here are some workers

fixing the track.

Here is the engineer

driving at night.

Here are the passengers

sound asleep.

Here is a railroad crossing.

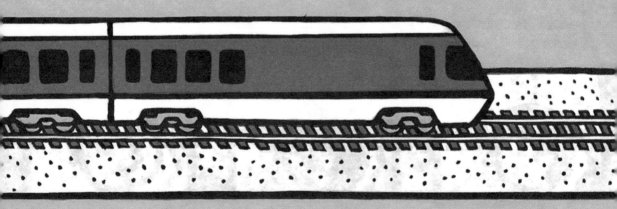

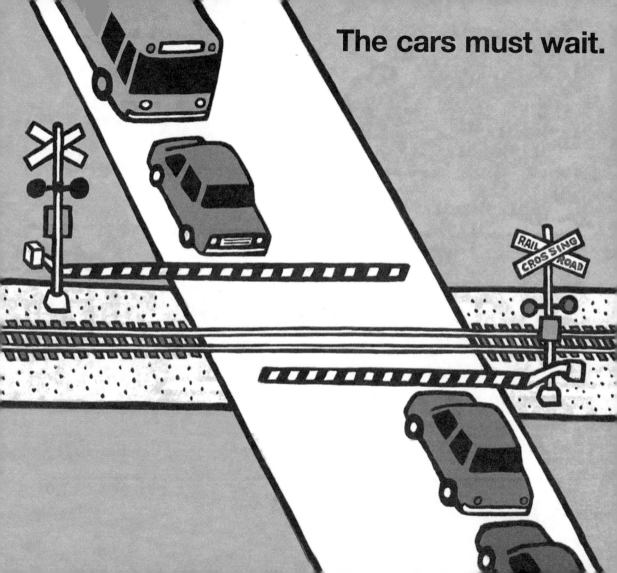

The cars must wait.

Here is a town.

The train passes by.

Here is a train station.

The train stops here.

Here are the people

getting on and off.

Here is the conductor calling,

There goes the train speeding away.